Gilgamesh

Also by Alan Wall:

Poetry

Jacob
Chronicle
Lenses
Alexander Pope at Twickenham

Fiction

Curved Light
Bless the Thief
Silent Conversations
The Lightning Cage
The School of Night
Richard Dadd in Bedlam
China
Sylvie's Riddle

Non-fiction

Writing Fiction

Gilgamesh

ALAN WALL

Shearsman Books
Exeter

First published in the United Kingdom in 2008 by
Shearsman Books Ltd
58 Velwell Road
Exeter EX4 4LD

www.shearsman.com

ISBN 978-1-905700-98-1

Copyright © Alan Wall, 2008.

The right of Alan Wall to be identified as the author of this work has been asserted by him in accordance with the Copyrights, Designs and Patents Act of 1988. All rights reserved.

Acknowledgements
'Jacob' first appeared in the book of that name, published by Bellew Publishing Company Ltd, London, in 1993. I am grateful to Marius Kociejowski for his invaluable assistance with 'Jacob'.

The author is grateful to the Royal Literary Fund for two RLF Teaching Fellowships, one at Warwick University and the other at Liverpool John Moores. He would also like to acknowledge the AHRB/Arts Council Fellowship he was awarded in 2003, to work with the particle physicist Goronwy Tudor Jones.

Contents

Gilgamesh	7
Jacob	49
Prologue	53
Part One: Nomads	55
Part Two: Man of Dreams	83
Part Three: Relatives and Singularities	99
Epilogue	118

*To the Memory of
Elizabeth and Michael Cavanagh
Beloved Grandparents*

GILGAMESH

Austen Layard and George Smith in Nineveh.

4,000 years after Gilgamesh had mourned for Enkidu
Two men knelt in the Babylonian dust
Tracing cuneiform inscriptions
And because of the wedged lines
Their fingers found that afternoon
Fellows in high hats in Piccadilly
Came to believe
God had not fashioned them from clay
On which had been inscribed the story of their life.

Dramatis Personae

Gilgamesh: *The great king of Uruk. Although born of a goddess, he was only two-thirds divine, and was therefore doomed to die. His humanity binds him to Enkidu, and prompts him to go in search of immortality. It is this which makes the original poem what Rilke called 'the first and greatest epic of the fear of death'.*

Enkidu: *He is the wild man whom the animals adore, until he begins to consort with humanity; then they turn away from him. The gods made him Gilgamesh's equal.*

Shamhat: *One of the temple prostitutes from Uruk, whose mission is to tempt Enkidu from his bond with the animals, so that he will side with humans.*

Ishtar: *Uruk's especial goddess. She commands the realms of love and war. Her favours can be as lethal as her displeasure.*

Huwawa: *The dreadful guardian of the Cedar Forest. His task is to protect timber for a god; then as now logging was a matter of life and death.*

Siduri: *A goddess of some considerable wisdom, who ran an alehouse on the far side of creation.*

Utnapishtim: *Noah's imaginative progenitor. He survived the universal inundation which drowned everyone else. He was reputed to hold the secret of immortality. Gilgamesh journeys to the other side of the world to find out if he does.*

1

Enkidu, the green man.
Enkidu, dressed in the skin of the forest.
He spoke the language of the animals;
Released them from their traps with his nimble fingers.
The creatures loved him.
The hunters didn't.
What shall we do? they said.
Our livelihood. This wild man
Is leaving our tables empty.

Hunters took their petition to Uruk
Where Gilgamesh, mightiest of kings, reigned supreme.
He raised a weary finger of command
And a new trap was set.
A hunter returned with a temple prostitute
Whose power kept Enkidu from fields,
Forests, rivers.
The dazzle of her breasts
Transmuted his power into juices
Flowing out of him and into her.

When they were done he went back to the animals
His oldest companions
But the gazelle turned and walked away.
Deer shook their heads, trembling, and departed.
Toad and rat vanished into hole and pond before him.
Even the wind, catching that scent and its ritual trade
Veered away quickly.
No animal would speak to him now:
He had passed beyond their language.
Seven days and seven nights with Shamhat
Meant that a new world awaited him.

He laid his bewilderment in her lap, and she told him:
You are as beautiful as the gods are now.
So go to Uruk where Gilgamesh, mightiest of kings,
Is waiting.

That night the king dreamed that a meteorite
Fell from the sky and he, who could lift anything,
Couldn't lift it.

Dreams were not dross in those days
And the king's mother told him:
The meteorite is a companion falling towards you.
A companion who will never leave you.

2

The goddess Aruru had made Enkidu
The other half of himself
Gilgamesh the king did not even know
Was missing—
Grass to his gold; snake to his torque;
River to his jewelled streams.
But Shamhat cut up her robe
Divided it between herself and Enkidu.
He whom the brothers and sisters of forest and grassland
Now shunned, was clothed finally, along with his harlot.
And Shamhat razored
The hair from his body.
Now Enkidu stepped from the trees to the city:
He was a man.
And when beer and cooked meats
Were placed before him
He stared at them as the animals had stared at him
Dressed in his new language.
The beer found a song inside him
Never sung before.

3

Now Gilgamesh slept with every beautiful bride
The night before her husband could take her.
He owned them all and took his possession—his birthright . . .
Her breasts, her thighs, the soft warm root
Leading down through the underworld, back up to heaven—
All these were the king's before the husband's.

Two-thirds divine, the other part human.
No one denied him.

But when Enkidu arrived in Uruk
On the day of the wedding, the people cried out:
Here is one mighty as the king
His shoulders, his back, the width of his arm
And a face from which a sun shines out.

Now the people of Uruk had wondered for some time
If Gilgamesh's world might be dying
Whatever his power.
He worked them half to death
Building the city's famous walls
Then let the walls decay for years
As though he'd forgotten the murderous labour
Involved in putting them up in the first place.
The whisky-breath, the silences
Colder than that ivory
Elephant he'd had them construct
Underwater, one grey November
When the gods weren't speaking.
Except for the nights when he slipped
Between sheets with the virgins
Gilgamesh spent most of his evenings

Speaking to gods. Mostly they didn't reply
Acknowledging the force of his own godly thoughts.

One night he saw
A camel become the sun
And could not explain it.
Even his favourite astronomer
Could not explain it
And soon beguiled himself
Instead with mathematics
Predicting the floods of the Tigris, Euphrates,
The Arno (1966)
The Severn and Avon in subsequent years:
The rise and decline of great dynasties.

The lion goes back to the mountain.
Enough of the world for now.
Enough. Gilgamesh felt this way all too often
As he stared at the stars above Sumer
Firing off billions of photons a second
But saying, in the process, very little.

So Gilgamesh had paid little enough attention
When this wild man's presence in the valleys
Was announced. Mere gossip for cuneiform columns.
He'd heard it all before:
Bigfoot in the forest of believers,
Loch Ness Monsters, divinities in flying saucers
Delivering the spores of life.
He yawned. Horoscopes bored him.
Almanacs and flaring comets bored him.
Now and then in the grey gauze of a December afternoon

He'd see an oakman in the palace shadows
One who could kill a warrior with a single rhyme.
Would he drop a commendation in my grave
Thought Gilgamesh, assuming that I can't escape it?

As a king you had to listen
Over and over again to witless words from *hoi polloi*.
How a goddess died in a concrete tunnel
While the lights of the world flashed upon her
A nation's hopes unresurrected in her womb.
The people mourned for a week on the vernal plain
Hardly a mile from the statue of Eros
And the steel shelves of the London Library.

Uruk had a library, of course,
The removal of any volume from which
Meant death. Unless you were Gilgamesh—
He had recently borrowed
A handsome biography
Of himself. In which
Enkidu as yet did not even
Merit a mention. As yet.

And now here he was
The half of himself Gilgamesh
Did not know was missing.
Here he was.

4

Enkidu stood before the bedchamber
Where the lady awaited the king
Who would enter her first, so her husband might follow.
And they fought.
Normal men would have died ten times over
From a single one of these blows.
No one died. Gilgamesh won.
Out in the street the people
Heard an earthquake thundering beneath them.

'Ninsun birthed you and said there could not be
Another one like you.'

Thus Enkidu, as they embraced.
That night Gilgamesh forgot to take
The other man's bride.

5

Enkidu speaks:

Huwawa is the guardian of the Cedar Forest.
When he breathes, a dragon's breath flares out
Scorching an acre with each methylated mouthful.
When he weeps
A county the size of Gloucestershire drowns.
When he frowns, men drop down dead in the next village.
Enter the Cedar Forest and you're finished.

And Gilgamesh:

Ever tried going to heaven, my friend?
Only gods arrive there.
If we are to exist, let's risk everything.
One of these days I'm off to the Cedar Forest
To fight Huwawa.
So follow and remember—
Our sons will one day sing songs about it.

6

Even with Enkidu near him
Gilgamesh had once more grown weary—
He consulted the oracle.

Wherever kings reside, oracles flourish:
Vienna Versailles Washington Jerusalem.
In Uruk they were blazoned in the Yellow Pages
Framed in enormous black boxes. And the oracle
Uttered his prophecy thus:

The lassitude which is often a king's fate
And which Baudelaire will address
4,000 years from now in Paris, is presently yours.
The poet Charles will be a most unroyal creature
Though a king of sorts with Jeanne Duval,
The creole whore who'll queen him
As they rise on hashish clouds
Through sundry darknesses in one arrondissement
After another. He will see precisely the same swan
You do today, my Lord, dragging white wings
Through the *trottoirs*. The poet, the king, the god.
Each of you crowned with dispossession
And all of you pointed, with compass precision,
At death.

Like the gnomon on a sundial
Turning sunlight to shadow.

For every hour is the hour of our death.

All right, said Gilgamesh, we go get Huwawa
Then every hour will be his no longer.
We're off to the Valley of the Shadow of Death,
Enkidu. Might be better if we both travel light.

7

The old men of the city shook their bald heads and muttered:

A young king, and a king in his glory
But Huwawa is the twin towers collapsing,
Aircraft falling out of the skies as the rapture seizes,
The belt of asbestos around a martyr's waist
For that last smile at the Israeli checkpoint.
He's Omega, although he speaks no language
Or only the last letter of each
Before darkness and silence get started.

Huwawa is the Hindenburg
Lakehurst, New Jersey, 1937
Lying down in its cradle of flame
A buckled skeleton
The ribcage of an airborne diplodocus
Evolution's gravity has crushed at last.
He's the fire next time.
Birds igniting in mid-air
Cats dogs squirrels foxes household rats
Hissing once so briefly
Then gone for ever from the firmament.
A whole city become a print
A photograph of its own death in an instant
Receiving the explosion's flash
As the sacred vessels crack and scatter light
No one ever saw before with such intensity.

Enola Gay, great shining bird
From aviation's bestiary
Flies home again to victory
Leaving implanted in those below

New wombs
Inextinguishable candles for the future's cave.

Brightness falls from the air.

So let Enkidu go first
Enkidu who has climbed inside the crocodile's jaw
Travelled through the dragon's gut
Slept salted inside shark and whale
Only to swim like a dolphin at dawn.

Let Enkidu lead him
To the green shadow of death that is Huwawa.
Let him navigate the fire and the ice
Of these, our coming ages.

8

Huwawa was hateful to the sun-god.
He was the shadow no sun should ever see.
Rimat-Ninsun, Gilgamesh's mother, prayed
That the god should protect her beloved
Resting his golden aurora, a perpetual benediction
On the head that had come out between her legs.
Covered in blood, even though two-parts a god.

According to Ezekiel, the Assyrian
Was a cedar in Lebanon.
Not anything like the cedar
Travelling by the name of Huwawa, he wasn't.

And the demon waited now,
Smelling rich food on the wind.
An Easter Island head of soft volcanic stone
Stares out towards a sea without a sail upon it.

9

When two men walk, day after day,
Even when one is almost a god,
They become one: their appetites are married,
Their hungers, their thirsts, even their words
Inseparable, a narrative skein
Not yet finally knotted and brushed free of dust
In the sunlight.
They had met at the threshold
Of a bride's chamber.
She had wept when the king that night
Omitted to touch her.
And so they walked on, sometimes laughing, sometimes silent,
Towards their meeting with Death.
'The distinguished thing,' Henry James called Death
Who had evidently not encountered Huwawa
In the Cedar Forest.

Like Sigmund and Lou-Andreas Salomé
They went for one another's dreams.
'That mountain falling is Huwawa.'
'The raven's your fear.'
'Water's the future flowing towards you.'
'The fish with a man's face is wisdom.'
'Then nothing can ever drown it.'

10

John of Patmos would borrow this:
Huwawa wore seven different veils of terror.
With all the lot on, you'd had it.
You were trapped in the Underground
Where he stored his explosives.
All you could see out there
Was the Flemish bond of the brickwork
Between King's Cross and the next dark station.
Gilgamesh and Enkidu
Slipped inside the Cedar Forest incognito
With Huwawa wearing only one
Of his black flags.
Even so. He breathed: mustard
Gas and anthrax came out
Thick as a factory cloud.
And it looked for a moment as though he had them.
Shouted so loud the sun blinked.
But finally they jumped him; hacked him to pieces.
Cut off his head and set off back to the city
Carrying the demon's head before them.

Only one thing, though: Enkidu was wounded.
Something from the shadow of that forest
Had entered his body and wouldn't come out.

This will make poetry one day, won't it?
Already some dutiful student
In the Scribal School high in the mountains
Is inventing a new rhyme for 'slaughter'.

11

According to Pliny, the Astomes
Lived on air; sweet odours
Provided all the sustenance they needed.
Roots, flowers, wild fruits in woods
Distilled a primal protein, which
Renewed them, so fine were their
Digestions and their palates.

    But should a stink
Emit from rotting lilies, scummy ponds,
Dead horses decomposing, roadside carrion,
A crocodile in Nile-sand, its open belly
Birthing ephemeridae,
Crowmeat, maggot meal, any feculent material
The air breathed and held in its blue
Lungs, then they were poisoned, these
Ariels of calibrated inhalation,
Eaters of aromatic breezes
And in coughing out mephitic matter
They coughed themselves out too
And died.

So Gilgamesh and his companion kept that head of Huwawa
    at a distance
Since Huwawa turned all men into Astomes.
First Gilgamesh then Enkidu held it
At arm's length
The way Perseus held Medusa's head
So others could freeze
Into polished granite, holding that pose then for ever.

The head was the herald of their barge
As they sailed slowly upriver
Back towards Uruk,
City of diamonds and wonder.
That head was enough
To turn June to December
In the city that never sleeps.

12

What happens next?

A weapon is a curious thing.
Designed to draw blood, it remains still,
While blood is upon it, tainted.
Gilgamesh wiped the darkening blood of Huwawa
From his blades.
Thick-hearted Huwawa, dressed in his trellis of zeroes,
Who's lost his way in time and space,
Even in the mirror of the forest of his life.

And that was when Ishtar saw him.
The goddess saw the demon's assassin
Washing blood out of his hair and blades
And scraping demon-vomit from his fingernails.

This one she wanted
His flesh-blade sheathed inside her flesh
As the metal one had sheathed inside Huwawa.

She promptly proposed:
Your seed inside me
My power combined with yours.
Dynasties will sprout from our contact
Like lichen on gravestones.
Come summer or winter
The seedings will flourish.
Our names will flower
As yews do when bones decay beneath them.

Queen of Love she might have been
She was also Queen of the Dark,

An underworld dealer. Each vein
Turned blue to black. Little wrappers of silver.

Ishtar had previous, where men were concerned,
And Gilgamesh knew it.
Tammuz. She'd had him all right, and where was he now?
Pushing up daisies.

Then Ishullana.
Come into my darkness, you said.
Think I'll stick with the light, if that's all right, he'd replied.
Now some say he's a frog
In slimy water.
Some say a mole
Blind as the earth.

Either way, Ishtar, these were hardly career moves he'd planned,
Now were they?

13

Ishtar consulted her father, Anu,
Capo di tutti capi of the skies,
And his doxy, Antum,
Whose *mores*, though feminine, after a fashion,
Were not all that much better than Anu's.

I need a hitman, parents;
An honour killing is required.
Your daughter has been jilted
By one only two-thirds a god.

You wanted him, the old man said.
If he'd already got your number and withheld his seed
So what?

The Bull of Heaven. Lucca Brazzi.
I want Gilgamesh killed.
Otherwise out come the dead.
I'll open the graveyards of hell.
Pol Pot will re-build your heavenly cities
With skulls instead of bricks and stones.
Heydrich and Himmler
Will come back dancing.
I'll turn your silken sleeping-sheets
Into Cambodia and Auschwitz.
The Bull. The hitman. Now.

14

Euphrates spilt itself in a raging tide
As Ishtar had wished Gilgamesh would
Inside her.
Uruk rattled with shock and awe.
The bull kept bellowing.
The White House microphones had been left on.

To dig one of these out of the mountain
Layard's workmen needed a trench
90 feet by 16 feet by 22.
Buffaloes wouldn't even pull the effigy that day.
And that was nothing but a tiny replica.
Imagine the actual bull of heaven, then,
Breaking with breath
What others could barely break with an axe.

What could be done?

Enkidu went for it.
The hitman, the Bull, was himself now the mark.
Death in the afternoon.
A blade right through the shoulderblades.

The bellowing sound an F-16 makes
Bringing its latest messages from heaven
To the land of the prophets below.

Once they'd both hacked him down
Gilgamesh and Enkidu walked
Hand in hand to the edge of the river.

How is your wound, my friend?
Has it started its healing?

No answer. Enkidu said nothing.

15

In the *battue*, beaters press lions on
Until they are netted. Tricky should one of your netsmen
Prove unsure of his knots.
Or if you set out by underestimating the lion.

The gods sit in council.
In an oval office they sit
With a Bible open at a page in Exodus
Describing salvation for a few;
Slaughter for many.

Huwawa dead.
The Bull, the hit-man, slaughtered.
How will this go down in heaven,
Amongst the statistics of apocalypse?
How should Halliburton calculate the outcome?
Will zeroes in ledger books burst their skins?

Surely Enkidu must die.
Gilgamesh is royal. He can live—
Say, Hirohito in 1945 on the Chrysanthemum Throne
While MacArthur makes all the running
Out there on Tokyo streets.
Like the Japanese, Babylonians obey orders:
Thus the wisdom from above, then as now.

They mutter darkly in conclave.
Papers are signed.
International calls are made, discreetly.
Men in suits speak softly in corners.

Suddenly Enkidu falls sick
Like Arafat, poisoned perhaps in his compound

Or Litvinenko lit up inside
By radiation's
Malevolent candle.
That wound from Huwawa
Had the essence of darkness inside it.

Enkidu:

It will be lonely in the grave
Between the Tigris and the Euphrates
Without you there smiling or shouting.
Saddam will be there, of course,
Entangled now with the spirits of his victims
Like a cat coming up from the cellar
Its face bejewelled
With gossamer from cobwebs.
Still, no point killing him twice.

And Gilgamesh:

I'd rather die than walk about up here without you.

Enkidu asked if no wisdom
Could be gleaned from the gods.
Gilgamesh turned his face towards the sky and squinnied.

'They're planning a catastrophe,' he said finally.

'Are we in it?'

'Everyone's in it. All whose names appear in the Book.'

Then Enkidu began to curse:

Let the hunter's fingers be broken in his traps.
Let the harlot Shamhat
Have her womb sealed
So that no life can go in
And none come out.

And Shamhat answered softly:

I gave myself to you. You were glad to have me then.
Why do you curse me now?
Why do men always curse
What they want so badly
When they cover you with kisses?

Then Enkidu:

Forgive me, Shamhat.
Let men die inside you each day
So others might live
The others they kill as soon as they leave your temple.

16

Lion head. Eagle talons.
Occluded face. Enkidu's dream
Bred from the fear in his belly.

A potsherd shaped once by fingers
Millennia back.
Human clay fashions its vessels
Then they sink down to the earth together
To be dug out by enterprising spirits;
Entrepreneurs of the grave.
Layard, Schliemann, Woolley, Smith.
Pottery, statuary, skulls—
Accepted by earth
As her due. But in time
All funerary cities resurrect as scholarly inventories
Inside museums.
Yorick's skull in Hamlet's bony hand.
Revenants leering from the emblem book.

2,800 years of undisturbed peace
Then 600 miles down the Tigris
12,000 miles via the Cape back to London
Where in the British Museum
An old man takes off his glasses and ponders.

Now I am a bird
Heading for the Graveyard Kingdom,
Stone meadows, rivers of sulphur.
There they swallow dirt, drink sewage,
Earth's bilge their sustenance.
And Gilgamesh, while all this was dreaming away inside me,
You did nothing.
You abandoned your friend to the badlands
Where even shadows must die.

17

These two, remember, had been partisans
Hidden away in caves
Hearing the squadrons advancing.
Ears pressed to short-wave radios
As quislings broadcast the nation's motto:
'Nothing we could do except collaborate, believe me.'
They'd stared along Hell's corridors
To see Austrian bankers, circa 1945,
Opening their manicured hands wide and intoning:
'Most of all we regret losing.'

Gilgamesh realised, after all this,
That he had betrayed his companion with despair.
Enkidu could do nothing now but die.

Gilgamesh placed a hand on his twin's heart
But the thunder there had ceased already.
The darkness in his wound had swallowed him.

So Gilgamesh:

Now the gazelles will speak to you again
Toad and rat nuzzle against you
Wrens nest in your hair.
Snakes will necklace you.
Old men with rheumy eyes will weep
In dusty grieving corners of Uruk.
On council estates girls with hidden tattooes
Will turn from their screens in silence.
A gem in the dusty earth will close
Its brilliant, glass eye.
A day will forget to dawn.

18

Gilgamesh brought his kingdom together.
His commands were as follows:
Let medals be struck
Beautiful as the Armada Victory of 1588
More valuable now than this tiara in my hand;
Let statues be constructed;
Poems be written and read
By laureates and gleemen;
Songs sung
By blind men with luthiers beside them;
Prayers recited in every language ever spoken.

Let cattle give birth to no calves
Sheep to no lambs.

Let anyone who sets sail this day
Drown.
Let men tremble.
Gods weep.

Enkidu, my beloved, is gone,
The half of me
I never even knew was missing.
Which, as of today, is missing once more.

And if he is gone, I'm next.
For who knows the road away from death?

19

Utnapishtim knew the road away from death
Though some claimed it had always been a by-pass,
Not an exit.

Gilgamesh went in search of him.
And found that though Enkidu might be dead
Lions weren't.
In the mountain passes he slept only fitfully.
Couldn't see more than a minute ahead
(After JFK's assassination you heard
Only the trembling bugle call,
The little boy raising his hand in obedient salute.
When the coffin goes into the ground
You follow.)

Utnapishtim. Yes. He had the answer.
So let's go meet him.
The king met a male and female dragon.
Even they were appalled at the thought of his journey
But didn't try to pull rank.
Instead they gave him some detailed directions.

Three tunnels there were.
The kind of tunnels people die in, even kings.
Tunnels that go round and round
And people spend eternity screaming inside them
(see Dante's Inferno, *passim*).

Now Gilgamesh's fear was a scorpion
Clutching a void between its two concave pincers.
He would have cried out, but what should he cry?
As they took one in the chest at Ypres
Soldiers would call upon Jesus.

Gilgamesh couldn't do this
For Jesus was still 2,000 years in the coming.
And there's no way of knowing what he would have made
Of the Nazarene's Aramaic litanies.
Simply too hard to say from this distance,
As it would have been from that.
Anyway, what he cried was 'Enkidu'.
But his friend wasn't there and couldn't help him.
Each valley was a wound now with a darkness inside it.

The third tunnel by this stage
Was a grave where the sun died daily.
It felt like Ishtar's womb
(Could she really have gained him at last?)
But beyond that, a garden
Whose trees fruited jewels,
The same ones Adam and Eve sat naming
Smiling at the syllables their tongues invented
One surreal market day in a Cotswolds Eden.

20

Now Esau was an hairy man.
So Jacob dressed himself in an animal's hide
Presenting this form to his blind (and senile)
Old father; thereby he won for himself the blessing
That should properly have been Esau's right.

All this you may read in Genesis
A book to come later
Vastly indebted to this one.

And thus did Madame Siduri, the tavern keeper
See a hairy man
Making his way along the shore:
Gilgamesh, two-thirds a god
(But only two-thirds, remember)
Dressed in an animal hide
Looking for all the world like Enkidu
After his first night out in the fields with Shamhat.

This hobo, this tramp, this dead-beat,
Dressed in the skin of a raw beast
She decided not to include in her Wednesday karaoke evening
And promptly locked all seven doors.
Gilgamesh shouted through the letter-box
Reminding the hostess
Of his list of slaughters and attainments,
Whatever the state of his kaftan these days.

If you're him, why do you look like that then?
You look like thirty bad winters
Chain-ganged to thirty dead springs.

Huwawa's joint assassin replied:

I watched a worm
Slide from Enkidu's nose,
My beloved, my faithful companion.
Enkidu who walked the earth
Is now earth himself;
Who ridiculed death has sunk in death's maw.
Who helped put Huwawa into the grave
Is now in the grave beside him.
So, tell me, what does that mean, exactly?

What awaits us?
Either hard earth or the waters of darkness.
Waters of death like Styx.
The Titanic, no bulk-heads in steerage.
Waters chewing your fingers
Like famished piranhas.

So what do we say?
Might as well eat, drink, and go to it
As if there's no tomorrow.
Phone up the harlots from the temple.

Except for one thing:
Might death be avoided?
Who should be consulted?
Whose shining glass tower-block
Along the Embankment
Contains this state secret?

21

British officers in 1943 out on the North Atlantic routes
Often looked first at the icy seas
Then at their freezing men on deck and wondered:
'Can I keep the two apart for long?'

So Gilgamesh sailed on through dark waters
Waters of death, seas of oblivion,
Until he came to Utnapishtim
Master of the greatest distance
Either on a mariner's chart or an Ordnance Survey map.
But when Gilgamesh looked at Utnapishtim
He saw a man
The man who had survived the Flood.

This man told Gilgamesh his story.
Living as he did on the other side of history, these days
He seldom had the chance to tell his story.
His wife had already heard it many times—
Having lived the story with him in the first place.

Forget global warming, he said. When the inundation comes
When the tide reaches your kitchen and your bedroom
You don't need analysis: you need a boat.
So build one.
Measure it in cubits if you like.
Whatever suits your calculator
And your tax return,
Not to mention your particular scribal tradition.
Two-thirds of the boat
Containing all the creatures worth keeping
Will be underwater.
From this day on, mankind will be
Effectively the offspring of fish

(Another man with a beard almost as long as mine
Will come along to confirm this in writing in 1859.)

Like Noah at a subsequent date—
'My clone, I fear'—he found himself
Wondering sometimes if
The whole of creation had been
Only by way of rehearsal.

After what seemed a lifetime
But was really a matter of weeks
A dove flew out from the boat and flew right back.
But when the raven was released he never returned.
Earth was drying out.
Soon all the birds swerved up off the ark and through the sky
Like starlings in a northern city square at twilight
Or electrons rushing down a cathode tube.

Ishtar came from heaven
With a breast-bone made of lapis lazuli
And stared at the survivors.
Enlil wondered out loud, enraged,
How this one boatful should escape disaster
Since all of life had been marked down for it—
As though a handful of kulaks should
Outlive the Ukraine famine
Or a small factory of Jews
With Schindler's name branded upon them
Should not breathe the gas
Their fathers and mothers, their sisters and brothers
All did breathe. Their last.

Still there were pairs of everything
To get creation started up again
Though one poisonous spider apparently
Impregnated herself:
Arachnoid parthenogenesis.

22

The test of the gods is this:
That Gilgamesh stay awake for seven days,
Then shall he hear from Utnapishtim
The secret of eternal life.

Now seven days is a long time to go without sleep
Even if you are two-thirds a god.
The disciples of Jesus couldn't last much longer
Than an hour, as their redeemer sweated blood
And conversed with angels—
They of course were human all the way through
As their non-appearance at the crucifixion
The following day would put beyond question.
Even so.

Gilgamesh was tired.
With Enkidu's death, with his own mighty travels.
In truth, with life itself.
He was exhausted. And he slept.
Seven days of sleep
Like Enkidu's seven days with the temple harlot.

Utnapishtim woke him gently and explained:
You didn't stay awake after all, my Lord.
So immortality is no longer an option, sadly.

But there was still something to hold on to:

A plant grows beneath the waves
Which makes old men young.
Borrow my snorkel for a day
And you'll most likely find it.

Gilgamesh tied stones to his feet
(Since lead boots along with divers' helmets
Were not yet invented)
And down he went.
Eels coiled around him,
But he found the plant
Which grants endless youth to the aged,
Smoothing out even the mind's wrinkles.
Its thorns cut his palms and his fingers.
Blood swirled up in clouds as he re-surfaced.
The tide's transfusion.

On the way back from the edge of the world
He put the plant on the leafy side
Of a pool while he bathed.
He was caked with salt;
Dry-skinned from his own local deluge.
Gleet had seeped through his pores.
He had, after all, crossed the sea of death
Which is dirty, dark, polluted.
A serpent, catching the plant's freakish fragrance,
This essence of youth,
Recipe for both birth and photosynthesis,
Made off with it
Leaving only one dead skin behind.

He stood and stared at his feet.
On the sands there a note had been written
In Enkidu's hand. I taught him that script,
Thought Gilgamesh. Now he has fallen
Through the hole of his death
Into the future.

Hell is well-lit, my friend.
We were there before New York or London.
The illumination here at night is skin
As phosphorus eats and erases it.
I send you these words from Fallujah
At the beginning of the end of history.
When you are sure you've got history started
Come and join me in the terminus.

23

With the boatman at last
As they entered Uruk alone together
The king said:

Look at that glorious brickwork
Gold on the windows
Statues of all the immortals,
Some even of Gilgamesh. Not a bad likeness.

Who's Gilgamesh? the boatman asked
Without turning round.

Look down at the coursing water, boatman.
That's your life and mine.
King and peasant, queen, priest,
Rower, gleeman, assassin of demons—
The waters flow on.

The waters flow on through our fingers.

JACOB

And Jacob said unto Pharaoh, The days of the years of my pilgrimage are an hundred and thirty years; few and evil have the days of the years of my life been, and have not attained unto the days of the years of the life of my fathers in the days of their pilgrimage.

Genesis

... once again, the fierce dispute,
Betwixt Damnation and impassion'd clay.

Keats

Every angel is terrible.

Rilke

Dramatis Personae

Jacob: *Patriarch circa 2000 B.C.*

Rachel: *His wife and his true love.*

Leah: *Also his wife and Rachel's sister but not his true love. He was tricked into taking her by Laban, her father, who wanted the elder sister off his hands.*

Isaac: *Jacob's father and Abraham's son. He whom Abraham was commanded to sacrifice to demonstrate his obedience to God's will. But the Lord stayed Abraham's hand.*

Rebekah: *Jacob's mother and Isaac's wife. Her tricksiness enables Jacob to receive the blessing intended for his brother.*

Esau: *Jacob's twin brother who loses both his birthright and his blessing to his younger rival.*

Jack Rose: *British poet, 1906–1972. The author of* Nomads. *In the latter half of his life he lived as a down-and-out in London's East End, where he died a vagrant.*

Ray: *1910–1991. Jack's wife and the mother of his two sons.*

Note: *Penuel was the spot where Jacob wrestled the angel.*

Prologue

Between his hungry women
and his uncommissioned dreams
between his wrestling bouts
and the next bleak session
at the psychotherapist's
between a dozen sons
and 12 tribes thriving
reckless in fecundity
between two wives
and their maidservants' bodies
between a brother's birthright
and his wrath
between the cryptic
noises of his car
and the sphinx-like
smiles of garagemen
pondering their strategies
between the odds
that anything he owns
still works
and the likelihood
it still might work
with much conviction
one month hence
between famine at home
and idols abroad
the limbs of the temptress
fleshed out for destruction
the far side of Canaan
between this unnamed
ravenous desire
and a fair chance of expressing it
upon sheets
or between them

Jacob stays broke.

PART ONE

Nomads

Jacob lives. The man and myth of *Genesis* is sleeping this night underneath the ladder that links earth to heaven, and he must wake again tomorrow to his own treachery. For Jacob betrayed his brother Esau to gain his birthright and blessing. He betrayed his blind old father Isaac too—with his mother Rebekah's connivance. His reward for all this betrayal and deceit is God's grace. For he struggles with the other kingdom, that vigorous contestant of darkness. And a new name is bestowed upon him, the name of a nation and a faith, the name of a future promised and a remembrance enjoined.

Jacob is entangled still, caressing the bruised membranes of folded wings. Above him are the stars in which is prefigured his fate and the fate of belief itself. Beneath him lies the crooked land of his brother's inheritance. His wives live on in enmity. His children extend the tradition of hate and dissension which Cain inaugurated not so long before. Sharp stones in their hands, lies in their mouths. Jacob is a fugitive from the fierce justice of his own family.

This is Jacob's book so it must be a book of treasons and of benedictions; of double-dealing and serenity. Jacob's pillow is the bleak stone comfort of insomnia, which he shares with every refugee scattered over the face of the earth. The only science he subscribes to is angelology: the physiognomy of luminous faces, the tracing (in the fastness of night) of the lineaments and terror of the holy. This fable of fecundity, our father, whom we must once more take up out of Egypt so he may sleep at last beside his ancestors' bones.

Plotter. Liar. Coward. Victim. Hero.

The corpuscles of dissimulation and courage contest equally within his blood. For here is a man blessed not with strength but cunning. It is Esau, his twin and predecessor, who has the strength. Jacob is wounded in his mysterious encounter with the angel, his night-time visitor. He carries the mark of his knowledge through the world as surely as Cain does his crime— one on the thigh, the other on the head. Rendered however not sterile thereby, but rather fecund.

Jacob, whose invisible ley line stretches even to Jack Rose, the poet (1906–1972), who stalks these pages too, dressed up in his own false skin. Jack, who abandoned his wife Ray for Leonora, then abandoned them both for the bottle. Who quietly froze one night by a canal in Wapping. Jack Rose who is the very fractured image of modernity itself, for all his angels have their faces turned away from him. Turned back into the future. So they may talk in their massive and unfathomable whispers. Leaving fragmentary instructions, runic traces in the sand, routes through the darkness.

Horoscope

>Always the quiet one
>humming softly to myself
>out there among the tentlines.
>'Mother's hairless little wonder'
>Esau would shout
>setting out with a grin to the slaughter.

>A real man, that one.

>They called me Rahamim
>my bride Shekinah.
>When we make love
>she weeps a kind of laughter.
>I laugh tears.

Ill-starred and blessed
by my own disposition
the wound that will hobble me still in the future.

I am here to adore what I'm torn from.
Creatures that come in the night
leaving on lethal wings at sunrise.

Visitors.
Dark ones with messages.

Though Jacob is technically the inferior of Esau, his elder twin who made it from the womb before him, yet it is he, not Esau, who is blessed. The blessing, like many blessings in scripture, involves pain and humiliation before eventual elevation is possible. Jacob has the future laid before him, one in which his seed will prosper. Among the phrases used originally of the horoscopist is 'a caster of nativities' and the horoscope proper is a scheme of the twelve houses or signs of the zodiac, like the twelve sons of Israel Jacob has prefigured to him.

Thomas Aquinas: 'A virtuous man can overcome even the stars'. Predictions are not fates. Jacob must still struggle.

CREDO

Shall we speak of my cunning
whose grandfather's dutiful hand
came within inches
of cutting the future's throat?
Here where the Lord of affliction and turmoil
gave me this wound
and thus blessed the world with asymmetry?

> The Lord who brought us this side of Euphrates
> out of the clutch of strange gods
> plucked Abraham out from the cult's devotees
> silverfleshed beneath torches at midnight
> to nothing but a still voice
> in a no man's land at night.
>
> Once spoken of course
> it's cunning no more.
> Admit with a poke or a smirk
> that blessing charade to old Esau
> he'd almost certainly not have gone hunting.
> Instead he'd have chided Rebekah
> 'You fond and foolish grey-haired old doxy'
> for unmotherly scheming
> then sizing me up like the fauna
> he spends his life sniffing and stalking
> he'd have smashed in my skull with a rock.
>
> So, shall we speak of my cunning?
>
> Not till the making of history's done with
> not till the memoirs get worked at
> massaged and revised after twilight each evening.

Odysseus is famously cunning but then he has many gods to placate. Jacob has only one—whose demands are unpredictable.

When Abraham was given Isaac, long after his wife had passed the age of childbearing, his life was renewed. Then Yahweh told him to take the child to Mount Moriah and offer him as a sacrifice. Abraham went to the mountain. And Isaac was spared by the Lord's mercy in the light of Abraham's obedience. But the lesson was plain: only because he is prepared to sacrifice

Isaac at the Lord's command does he get to keep him. A lesson lost again each generation.

Jacob cannot justify the tangle of his life (any more than can Jack Rose). And two and a half millennia before St Augustine invented the autobiography he probably had no urge to. In any case he might have been economical with the truth, if only to conserve his energy for the years ahead.

And he invented asymmetry because the world is no longer held in place by the counterbalanced weights of competing deities but by the one true power, explosive, real, unknowable except through endurance.

His Courtship

>Dolled up in the skin of a slaughtered goat
>hirsute for my old man's blessing.
>
>Before my dim-eyed father I have stood disguised.
>Even my wife brought to me veiled
>not, as it transpires
>the one I'd ordered.

Laban tricked Jacob. The father of Rachel was also the father of Leah, her elder sister. There were certain dynastic proprieties to be observed. So Laban substituted Leah for the promised Rachel.

But Jacob would surely have noticed—by a dip of the head, an inclination of the shoulder, the sheen of the hair or the lilt of the voice—some dissonance between his beloved Rachel and the impostor.

But not until morning . . .

At night it seems Jacob is unfettered from the chains of the expected. Despite the years of work still ahead of him before he finally reaches Rachel, he is secretly proud. Jacob has invented imagination.

Life from now on can become *(in extremis)* metaphorical.

It is of course one thing to be metaphorical. Quite another to be metaphor. What fate awaits Leah, loved as Rachel only until morning? She has brought, at her father's bidding, deceit into marriage.

Jacob's nemesis: the younger taking precedence over the elder. Yet here the process is reversed. The words of *Genesis* tell us that Leah's eyes were not bright. Which will help her as time goes on to see unreality steadily in place of truth.

There was a great deal of laughter up and down the land on the morning after the wedding. Laban congratulated himself on outmanoeuvring the cunning young Jacob. Rachel wept.

Leah

    With Jacob so deep in his wine
    I could have been anyone in his tent that night
    his fingers all over me
    blurring my edges.

    Dawn unsealed his eyes.
    I betrayed him with breasts, thighs, a snaking tongue.
    Counterfeit brought him
    to that furrow, Rachel's he believed.

For one night at least I was loved the way she is.
(He was promised Laban's daughter.
That much if no more was true.)
Later perhaps he might find in the nights I'm allotted
Leah has ways with her Rachel can't follow.

I count up my dreams, her years.

Old at thirty.

Wrinkling weirdly under the mounting sun.

We are given no real information regarding Jacob's feelings as to his ruinous deception, so we can only imagine:

Fix

I knew a man once made a pact with God
About a woman.
It was the wrong pact, the wrong woman.
Not even, it transpires, with God.
So this man, this fellow
(the one that I know)
sent out for the Boys with the Index,
the hieroglyph readers, the agents.

They came with their sky charts and codices
sucking the air through their teeth
and clicking their tongues
hunting through fact sheets and horoscopes
checking photographs dates the hour of conception
texture of hair and favourite colour
football team tax code
dentures and whether the parting is left right or centre

    any odd quirks in the bedroom
    recorded allegiance to outlawed political parties
    to search out some fissure, some fracture
    some hairline mistake in the scheme of his life.
    As though a thin crack grinning its way through the dyke
    should flood a whole country.

    They could not find anything.
    So they banished his dreams
    wrapped a luminous bandage
    right round his memory.

The Boys with the Index have their different incarnations through the years. Rabbinic, priestly, political, astrological. Whether in Roman Palestine, Tudor England or Stalin's Russia, their role remains the same. They have the truth. And the means for its imposition.

No one escapes whipping. Except of course for the analysts, the Boys with the Index, the hieroglyph readers, the agents.

Anyway, having no alternative, Jacob consults them as shall Jack Rose. Where does the trouble begin? Herr Doktor, kindly diagnose the enigmatic figure of my genesis. Put a name to the shape I struggle with.

His Conjunctions

    And never let you go unless you bless me
    who wrestled me into this corner, stranger
    keeping me so in the dark I haven't slept
    a decent sleep since I first set my hand
    on a black feather and dreamed blue sky.
    When you walk in the dust that surrounds me

    trailing your grand silken wings like a bride
    a fabulous bird some Egyptian invented for money
    is it really your choice this constraint of my body
    pulling you down into clay and derision?

    Or are you a messenger
    delivering me, the flesh of your mission?

    Daybreak absolves you always.
    You swerve clean away from my queries
    like an adulterer making the back door on tiptoe
    at first light after another haphazard
    strenuous coupling

    to be repeated, when exactly?

There is a rabbinic quality to Samuel Johnson's comment on the life of the poet, Christopher Smart: 'Madness frequently discovers itself merely by unnecessary deviation from the usual modes of the world. My poor friend Kit Smart shewed the disturbance of his mind, by falling upon his knees and saying his prayers in the street, or in another unusual place. Now although, rationally speaking, it is greater madness not to pray at all, than to pray as Smart did, I am afraid there are so many who do not pray, that their understanding is not called into question.'

Jacob was ridiculed too when he put into words what his nights contained. Such is the folly of any contrary faith. Invariably prompting laughter up and down the land. A chorus of acid voices dissolving anything solid.

Agon

Limping past Penuel, the sun rising
freighted at last with a serious name.

Condemned now to struggle
to wrestle those lofty and low ones
into the light.

Blessed be He
who appeared to my grandfather
by the terebinths of Mamre.

Who makes old barren women conceive
then orders the firstborn's slaying
only to stay his own fearsome hand.

Who frisked all Sodom for ten just men
just because Abraham bickered.

Who does not ask for silence
or a face tossed down like a plate in the dust.
He awaits man's word.

In enormous attendance
He waits.

Jacob had already grasped Esau's heel while still in his mother's womb. He strives even prenatally for blessings and birthrights. Esau is doomed.

Coarse, hairy, hunting Esau is doomed to be bested by his intellectual brother. The Lord has ever ordained it thus. The hunter shall find less and less of woods to hunt in. The pastoralists shall rule the earth, until the industrialists come along to rule them.

It is difficult to see why Esau should be on good terms with anything. His mother and brother combine forces to cheat him. His father prefers him, but is too blind to effect his preference. Even the Lord it appears has only made him first in order to rob from him all that is rightly his.

So Esau kills, getting better at it every day. And he has the nights in which to plot his vengeance. While Jacob is off somewhere meeting angels.

Esau

> I kill things.
> It's a kind of gift.
>
> With arrows knives water and stone.
> In my darkest moods
> with my own red hands
> feeling the warm life choking and sobbing
> its sad little tale
> till the carcass with its breath squeezed out
> sags slack against me.
>
> I pat the bristle and say:
> One day soon I will kill Jacob
> slowly.

Isaac, the father of Esau and Jacob, seems nearest to one free from sin. He who set off to Moriah with Abraham, his own father, to be the firstborn sacrifice. There is mystery, depths unfathomable, at the heart of him. What did he make of it all?

Abraham was called to make the sacrifice, but Isaac was to die.
It did not happen. But his father was there above him with the
knife in his hand.

REBEKAH

I have betrayed him, my Isaac.
But what would *you* do with a man
who prefers Esau to Jacob?
Almost blind and three-quarters deaf
says he hears no words now but the Lord's.

It's his father I blame.
My Isaac was a thin sliver of child
when they hiked off that day
with food hampers full
to a sacrifice up on the hill
which turned out to be him.

What did he make of it all?
Dad hears a voice saying:
'Go take your son, your beloved, and kill him'?

Sometimes I think that in Esau's fierce dark,
in the murderous black ice of our other boy's mind
he finds something that pulls him
back to that morning's sunshine
with the fire and the knife in Abraham's hand
and the sour metal taste of fear in his mouth
on that hillside.

Kierkegaard said that when he pondered the life of Abraham he was virtually annihilated by the monstrous paradox out of which it was constituted. It was the same annihilation Rilke speaks of in the *Duino Elegies*—the annihilation that would be visited upon us should we be embraced by an angel. The same messenger arrives on different wings.

Isaac

Esau had a thought—
the only one I have ever known blossom
in the dark weather of his mind.

He says my wife schemed the whole thing
that Jacob's too shiftless and moony
to ever have planned it alone.

And he's right.

Inches in front of my nose the treacheries flourish—
my eyes see nothing.

No sound of masonry crashing.
No rain clouds gathering, no dark voice
come for the reckoning.
No angel appears to pull someone's hand from the cut
no damp splodges starting to mottle the earth.

And He says?

One thing Isaac finally understood: the knife was still at his throat. He was awaiting always the ram in the thicket. Praying for an angel to come. Praying for the lethal manoeuvres of men, however inspired, to end.

Such signs might be taken for wonders. Sometimes rightly. Sometimes not.

As the rains drove down, lifting the ark gently at first towards the sky, one of the Index Boys sat with a damp scroll on his lap explaining patiently how this particular event was not predicted and therefore could not last. A blip, no more, in an otherwise faultless summer.

As the Church's exegetes explained to Galileo: If theology does not convince you then surely common sense will. Simply watch the star rise over the stable.

As the newspapers explained in 1914, the boys will come laughing home by Christmas.

As diplomats the length and breadth of Europe explained to their presidents, monarchs and wives that one landscape-painting corporal could not possibly intend what he so clearly stated in *Mein Kampf.*

As the treasonous clerks of the West explained in their smart periodicals that Uncle Joe could not possibly wish the annihilation of the Bolshevik old guard, not to mention half the peasantry of the grey empire over which he presided.

As doubtless, when Armageddon gets started, a well-groomed young man on a late-night television programme will elicit from a retired general that this is no more than a little local difficulty in the Middle East.

Sometimes signs are taken for wonders. Other times both signs and wonders are completely ignored.

Meteorology

I've told them again and again. I say:
Watch it.
It won't do to take His word lightly.

My grandfather talked Him out of it but one time
so sick of his miscreant creatures was He
that he drowned them entirely, one old sailor left
to bob on the briny, all creation paired off
midships on his groaning timber.

A solitary dove sets out each evening
but finding a drenched unhomely place
wings it back again at dawn
to nest in the fetid barge among strange fellows.

If you listen to the waves you'll hear
the elephant's dark turmoil
or the snap of a crocodile's insomnia.
Lions are fretting at this lying down with lambs.
All the animals are fraught with chaste confinement
and this is not the time to find monogamy
unsuited to your particular requirements.

A jealous God?

No-one with a serious interest in the climate
round these parts has ever doubted it.

Weathermen, zoologists (weak swimmers all of them)
trace runes in everything: sea, sand or sky
the least disturbance amongst gathering clouds.

★

Jack Rose's career to date?

Nomads. Published: London 1947.
Deleted from all lists in 1949.

Jack Rose spent ten years composing *Nomads,* the poem which he believed had located the missing heart of modern humanity. On the day of its publication he felt briefly as if he had given birth to himself in a second, more successful, operation. What happened? Nothing at all.

Jack decided at this point he was a man born out of his time. A time which in any case had replaced Kairos with Chronos. Chronos did not nourish his children. He ate them.

OUTLAWED

Jack the thief.
What has he stolen?

An old man's pair of eyes.
And Ray his wife's blind love
she would never have given
had she seen
one inch of the acres of black
stacked anthracite
blindness folded around him.

Some thief.

Jacob is beyond the pale. The wrong side of civilised. He has taken things to which he had no right. He ends up with things for which he has no longing. Leah for example. Those who are outside the law know only one protection: love.

To Rachel, Jacob is not cunning. At night with her, flesh to flesh, he has no more cunning than a newborn child. He rests inside her wound and is absolved.

The wound is the traditional place of refuge. In the middle ages the altars of certain churches afforded a refuge for fleeing criminals: 'In tua vulnera absconde me': in your wounds hide me. It is in vulnerability (that which is wounded or is capable of being wounded) that mercy is found.

But come the dawn it starts again: the mighty and lethal procession of his memories.

Quarry

In the quarry at the back of our estate
lettered hugely in white paint
nicked from a builder's yard somewhere
JACKO RULES
daubed up there by some local tyro
to intimidate the witless and attract the meek.

On drizzling Sundays
Jack would slouch that way to sit in perfect gloom
in a tented cave cut into the friable rock.

The quarrymen long gone.
The drills the dynamite.
Lorries dribbling shale and fossil
at the sharp turning into the road.

Occasional lovers under a weak moon
fumble fiercely down among
piss smells and broken bottles

hunting warm flesh beneath winter woollens.
The police have stopped calling
unless searching for a child's ragged body
after the latest ritual outrage.

As they might, mind you, just might
 have hunted out my father's father
in damp stony places
splashed with the blood of the first-born
muttering blackly, Wait till we catch
that murderous old bastard

had not the angel of the Lord
stayed Abraham's frail hand
the blade already poised to cut
deep into the body of his one beloved son.

The advantage of the nomadic life is also its greatest burden: not only can they move on, they must.

To the author of *Nomads* this injunction was not dictated by grazing tracks, but simple bloody-minded desperation. Jack Rose retired to Yorkshire *en famille*. The disappearance of *Nomads* into the black hole which fate prepared for it had stolen his enthusiasm for life.

He took to brooding in a nearby quarry. And after he had finished brooding in the quarry he went and brooded some more in the pub. Where he learned to play darts. Or, as the locals had it, throw arrows. Would that he could have poisoned a few of their tips, then flighted them back to specific locations in London (where his reviews had not been good).

Polygamy

It is not all evenings of wine, silk caresses
days of sultry adoration
long-nailed fingers tracing your rib-cage
their soft flesh proffered
ready for you to ponder
which of their breasts you'd like to fondle next.

Apologies and dreams, no more.
Shepherdesses are practical women.
(There's no flies for example on Leah
and the flies that squabble on Leah's slave girl
will be dead flies a few minutes later.)

On come the Boys with the Index:
'One woman is much like another.
So why in Brother Occam's words
multiply the entities without necessity?'

Fine, I say, except it's not me
in charge of the multiplication.
Leah for one arrived in my bed
after a family mix-up
regarding the wedding arrangements.
Well that's what she *says* ...

Now each time a problem arises they liquor me up
and I wake with a fresh face
beaming away on my pillow
as one who'd say:

'Did you enjoy that, Jack?
You certainly seemed to.
I'll start making lists now of a few things that *I'd* like...

As polygamy was gradually replaced by serial monogamy, men and women would promise to be faithful to each other until they did not feel like it any more. Then after a while they would promise to be faithful to someone else. And sometimes they would be. Sometimes not. No necessary limit to this sequence but the years of a life.

So many variants on this weary theme. One of the commonest and tritest is the older man falling for the younger woman and leaving the mother of his children to join her. Jack Rose did exactly that.

RAY TO JACK

I heard about Leonora by the way
the intellectual tart from the *Dog and Gun*.
I had wondered if her disappearance
coinciding as it did with yours
might have some significance.

What was it Jack?
Her fretless composure, that quality you so admire?
Her grasp of Pound's metrics perhaps—
possibly the convenience of her house in London
not to mention the 30 years you knocked off
when you traded me in?

I had noticed on our nights down there
how ripely she was packed inside her bra—
a fact presumably not lost on you
as you made her pretty head spin
with your dazzling insights into Milton.
I wondered why you suddenly started playing the poet again
instead of darts.

Now they say she got the boot as well.
Or was it the other way round?

And I hear you live rough sometimes.
You're no chicken, Jack.
We both have one foot in the grave.

Jack never replied to Ray's letters because he could not bring himself to concentrate on who she was. And what he had done to her. And what he had failed to do.

Jack and Leonora did not last long. But Jack Rose did not go home. He had fallen out of his home now for ever. He was back again on the streets of London and even angrier than before.

Mask

When Jacob first lapsed into my flesh
he murmured 'Rachel'
that bitch of a younger sister of mine
they all of them fell for.
Even our father himself, that mist-bearded
proprietorial dynast
only pushed me, tricked up in veils and disguises
into Jack's bed so he could hang on to his sweetheart
a little while longer.

But now when Jack looks at her
at the end of another seven years' promise and labour
he turns back to my body and my new technique.
He doesn't want those stupid curves
she's graced with.

> I visited the shrine and bought a charm.
> I had it fitted by the priest
> stained with Baal's perfume.
> I've started doing things with him down there
> she'd never even dream of
> with her hours of prayer. Her silences and meditations.
> She'll run to fat soon and he will exult
> in my hard little body
> bones quite visible out of my haunches.

Could Leah have been one of the world's first anorexics? It seemed to Jacob that on certain nights she made herself invulnerable by making her flesh invisible.

RACHEL

> I have looked on men.
>
> I see the holes in their faces
> they wish to keep hidden
> snakes coiled ready inside them.
>
> I see the well of quicksilver
> where they drown their oppression.
>
> But when first I saw Jacob
> I saw nothing at all
> but his hunger for me.
>
> So much desire
> Makes a man almost pure.

There is nothing in men, in their strutting and brutal persuasiveness, which Rachel has not already registered. Of

Jacob himself, his fear and deceit, his hunger to possess the future—all these she noted at a glance.

She has a grasping scheming father. She has a murderously deceitful sister who has poisoned the wells of the imagination with mendacity. Yet on certain mornings with the sun behind her it still seems as if Rachel can look at the world, see it clearly and whole, and still love.

In this she is surely Jacob's redemption, a fact even he occasionally remembers.

Snakes

> Almost impossible to ascertain their sex
> but Leah keeps one she always calls sister.
> She feeds it live rats and frogs
> she's cultured herself from the spawn.
>
> As you watch them go down
> wriggling and writhing in protest
> down through that slithering whiplash of gullet
> it's like a birth running backwards
>
> as Leah mumbles some dark hocus pocus.

It starts in the Garden of Eden as do a number of other things. From that point on snakes are no one's favourite. They slither and slide, their tongue splits down the centre of the truth. They reverse the natural order of things. As did Jacob with Esau. As did Leah with Jacob. Leah enjoys the way they swallow without mastication. She enjoys seeing the shape of the creature going down to destruction. And in one tradition the snake had legs before he tempted Eve in the garden. So he could be seen as the very figure of the fall itself.

Chaos

The serpent uncoiled and made for his favourite tree.

No stopping then, wholesale slaughter
the destruction of cities
till all that is left of the business
is Noah adrift on the wash
watching his planks warp, counting the days
hearing groans and complaints from the creatures in steerage.

You cannot heal it, you can only endure it
that atom, that spoor of a virus
which infected its way
out of the waters and into the veins.
I watch Leah journeying back
to the room in her heart
where she feeds snakes and rats with her poison.

I see her lips murmur 'Rachel'.

They are vulnerable—all who call out in the night and hold converse with angels.

Ray to Jack

I had to take your father for some glasses.
He can hardly see a thing. He calls Joe Ben, and Ben Joe.
Probably thinks that I'm the milkman.
He says you've robbed him of the peace of his old age, Jack.

The boys would like to see you.
I told them to save up for sleeping bags
or book themselves in at the Sally Army Hostel.

The dog still misses you as well.
But since she's three quarters blind
and nearly bald now from alopecia
she has more excuse than I do.

I gather they've reprinted *Nomads*
and that you are now the centre of a cult.
What cult is that Jack of which you are the centre?
And what does that make us, your distant family?

Leonora sent me a picture of you.
Vagrants living at the side of a canal.
Winter's coming on, you know. Have a care.

Your ever-loving
(evidently half-demented)

Ray.

Dido took in Aeneas and his Trojans saying that she had learnt to succour the unfortunate. And so effective was the succour she gave that Aeneas seemed happy to stay. It looked as though Rome might never get started. So Jupiter despatched Mercury to recall Aeneas to his high destiny.

Whatever prompted Jack Rose to widow his wife not by his death but his absence, it was certainly neither Jupiter nor Mercury. But off he went buffeted about on his own troubled seas.

No smoke arose from Sheffield that day, except the usual stuff from the steelworks. It was not like Carthage. Ray did not burn on a pyre.

She carried on living.

But felt still that half of her had been removed. Without anaesthetic. Or purpose. Or even some measure of courtesy.

Left

It is not the sorrow of the widow
curtaining the window with her breath.

Not the sea fragrance of that last September
when he worked on his unfinished opus
and stared at my thighs as gulls screamed.

Not jasmine on stone or the lady's one tear
salt and prismatic
while troubadors number the veins on the linden leaf.

It is not even the date of expiry
smudged in blue
on the municipal sticker inside the Mills and Boon.

It is to watch his future shift
like furniture from one house to another.

To hear another woman roll in her sleep on my years
as though they were sheets, freshly laundered.

To feel my legs
without him between them.

To watch this book slammed shut so heavily.

For what?

PART TWO

Man of Dreams

Jack broke his vows and then forgot about them. Or tried to. In this he merely contoured the lineaments of his age. Marriage, after all, is no more than history intimately written. And the time was not merely out of joint. Its spine was broken. That was how the Russian poet Mandelshtam saw it. He stared out from his imprisonment to see the ravening maw of unreason in an age lit with a greater welter of miscellaneous reasons than there were stars blinking across the heavens.

JACK BACK IN PRINT

Historic scars describe
her breasts, that V of bone hair
is the black hole of his dark return—

he comes out tiny and unsure
after she's done with him.
Something to be bandaged tenderly

something to be put back
into books, between the capital's fresh start
and stop's abandonment

or even the blithe comma teasing
bending over backwards to enquire
if that evacuation

left him safe and empty.

Where has Jack gone? Not to contentment surely? He has vanished back into the city of the modern. He had to go somewhere. If out of Ray and her *vulnera* then into Leonara instead; if out of Yorkshire then back into London; if out of the whole then into the fractured; if out of his ancient loyalties of the heart then into new disloyalties of the same organ.

He must be dreaming surely? Jack must surely have dreamt this. He's had grand dreams before. He's only six years younger than the century that spawned him, spreadeagled there with its broken back. And he's dreamed its dreams along with it. Each time he blinked a fresh apocalypse got started.

What after all was Jack Rose made of? Dreams? Science? Revolution? Poetry? Most certainly he did not know himself. And lost all the distinctions between them. Here for example are two of his dream poems of scientific revolution. And Jack most certainly dreamed revolution for a time, along with the century. With Lysenko he dreamed of wheat in the Arctic.

ONE OF JACK'S TWO DREAMS

He's making notes on revolutions
with such care. Only to see them get laid by
through winter's speechless months.

It's January probably, there's a January sky
but every window's open to the storm.
Just think of it, a study bright with snow

and you shovelling like mad to keep warm
after those plans for a book
crucial pages caught in the drift.

Then fastened by a cry so familiar you look
to see the sun
(a dead disc in the sky's nickel)

illuminate deserted steppes.

The Other One

Now he is this refugee
sometime in the thirties
scurrying through European capitals.

Not exactly Jewish
not Aryan either, enough books
in his bag to nail him.

Prophetically bearded he must cross
a blank deserted street.
Catches his reflection in a window:

A face dusty with sleep
a vagrant's pallor
queasy in dawn's gravity

captures an instant
fleck against grain:

A memory of his father sloshed
steering at the house in early mist
home again (but to which son, and which inheritance?)

Jacob too was torn from his family and from his twin. When Esau went from him so, in a sense, did the earth. He could not even lay his head on the ground from now on without opening up the heavens. His family replaced by a wound. A yearning for a brotherhood no future could imperil, no lie disinherit.

Fraternity

I address you as the owner of this sphere
who out of your own sleeping heart
have conjured a ladder fashioned from days.
Should I begin to call you brother?

Already you see yourself out on the hill
the provider of venison, beginning to wonder
if I'm all I'm cracked up to be.
And who on earth is that you ask yourself

kneeling underneath my father's hands
whose head in the skein of his beard
like a torn beast tangled in brushwood?
My hairs are not the beast's hairs . . .

It is of the essence of fraternities to betray themselves. The revolutionary brotherhood sooner or later fissures with a knife in the back or a bullet through the skull. The brothers of *Genesis* warned us of what was to come: murder, deceit, enmity, disinheritance.

False fraternity is perhaps the greatest curse of our time, leading to murder and something even more destructive than murder: a life fabricated entirely out of lies. The triggered knee-bending of Stalin's Russian Empire, Hitler's genocidal Reich, Pol Pot's Kampuchea, Ceausescu's tawdry, imagination-abolishing Rumania. Fresh candidates are queueing at the door, even as we speak.

False fraternity produces the over-ready hand-shake. The automatic testimonial. The good review of the bad book. The false appointment. The deceitful marriage. The betrayed child. False fraternity produces mendacity, which is always at the heart of every lethal social machinery.

False fraternity is based on fear. It is hard to speak the truth—as Isaiah knew, as Ezekiel knew, as Daniel knew. Jacob knew it too, liar though he undoubtedly was. Jacob sought reconciliation with Esau—he was at heart a family man. But he was truly afeared of Esau's murderous adroitness.

But still we fashion our dreams of harmony, our five-year plans, our thousand-year Reichs... There's probably someone plotting back home even now, while we're out hunting on the hill.

Esau's tragedy is really his mother. Jacob, left to his own devices, would probably not have amounted to much. But a mother prepared to betray her husband and her son means that Esau must live in a world of curses.

Gemini

A figure dances naked on ploughed sand
dances on his one good leg
above the furrows hieroglyphs and stones.
He carouses tonight under a double star
(two genial waltzers flaring in orbit)
and shouts loudly out to the shrivelling lights
what was whispered in one of his ears
this moonman, how his seed, his dark side of the bargain
shall spread to outnumber the scattered shiners:

Despite earth's shadow
predicatably sprinkled with omens

in the teeth of the blackouts to come
and in spite of his own frenzied swoopings
thrashing moist dunes where he grappled the stranger

>he starts with the driest of throats
>to swallow that promise.

Amongst the traditional twinned pairs which cluster about the sign of Gemini, Jacob and Esau form a troublesome duo. The twins can represent a wholeness lost to the bifurcation of sexuality or they can represent opposition, conflict, contradiction. Jacob and Esau are obviously not mutually reflective parts of a self-satisfied whole. They struggle one with another, not unto death but birth.

In the psychological trope which the Gemini sign often figures, the twins of opposition represent interior struggle, splitting, the acknowledgement by the forces of light of their opposite. Hairy, dark-minded Esau would thus be Mr Hyde to Jacob's Dr Jekyll.

The ability to hold two contradictory thoughts in the mind without either seeking to resolve them or going insane is, it has been claimed, a sign of genius. If this were true then Jack had genius, for not only must he hold on to two contradictory ideas, but two contradictory wives as well.

NOMADS

>Bad winds scathing the tent flaps
>night winds seared through with an unearthly cold.
>The beasts mournful, sullen.
>
>Leah stares at Rachel
>as I once saw Esau stare at a deer
>sniffing the air suspiciously, one hoof twitching
>before the arrow smashed the surface of that great moist eye
>and the creature creaked down stumbling to its knees.

We hunch in the murk of the swirls
and say nothing, mouths full of sand.

Every star dead.

Choices are sacrifices. We cannot have it all. Yet in a curious way Jacob gets it all—Leah as well as Rachel.

And he pays for taking what he did not choose. Oh how he pays.

Midrash

Time does not make ancient good uncouth
but with a little glossing
all too relevant
angled back towards the latest wound
the exact point of its suppuration.

Leah claims her wound has precedence.

How can a wound have precedence?

Through scrolls and codices
the Index Boys hunt and murmur
checking on this one.

They finally light on a law, old, immutable:

Leah has failed
to grow through her wound to her blessing.
Because of her plaintive and piteous whinings
her wound must stay curse now
unless she repents.

But Leah would rather rewrite the Torah in blood
using nails and teeth as a stylus
than bend.

She says: 'They're no good, those boys you brought in
they're too young and spotty.
What do they know, and what did you pay them?'

But Rachel believes them.
She saw from the start that her wound was a blessing
a focus to grow through.

Look at her now in the sunset
big at last with a child of her own.

Leah cannot face the fact of Jacob's love for Rachel. If she could face it, Jacob might well grow to love her too. But she would rather abolish the whole of creation than acknowledge that she does not have first place in it. She is an antithetical type to Rachel. For Leah would manipulate the heavens for her profit. In that lies the gravity and peril of her condition.

Jacob in Orbit

On the road to the stars
cleaning invisible windows
from my ladder

angel

I see this little ball
blue as a fresh baby's veins
that turns in the dark

>oh my angel

>and is spinning
>already
>from His hand.

Jacob's visionary dream in Bethel led to the place becoming a cultic centre until it was destroyed by Josiah. Dreams have potent legacies. They become that fissure inside our earthly completion whereby we let in the light.

Whether Jacob's mental journeyings can be compassed by purely earthly means, in metal canisters propelled through space by a distillation of human ingenuity, remains to be seen. In the films they send back the earth still seems to be entirely innocent and entirely beautiful. At that distance, though, people are invisible. Like angels when they choose.

In any case the time is out of joint, like Jacob's hip. How diagnose the lineaments of his struggle?

RISING FROM THAT LEATHER COUCH

>Now when a man rises, limping up
>from the couch of his wound and bereavement
>soliciting blessings from out of his fractured desires
>from brother, father, all whom he's wronged
>what is the difference in price
>whether that couch is of medical leather
>fringed by the Herr Doktor's ottoman
>or merely sand round Penuel
>furrowed with death marks?
>(Clinging to one another's heels we

fight our way out of the womb
to climb upwards again on a prayer
whose eyes are the sun, whose voice a stilled wind)

Peace there will be at last among the angelic orders.
Among thrones and principalities.
Even up there in the shining cities of men.

The one and the many. The many and the one. And how we might one day reconcile them. It should be said that our efforts here over the last century do not inspire confidence.

NIGHTFALL

Tell me now what heals men's hearts.

The black widow grins
and chews over these things with her lover.

And a night as silky
as a cockroach shell
has tightened across this land.

I remember nothing
but lies, betrayals and hurts.
But tell me, do, what heals men's hearts.

I'll buy some.

The black apocalypse or vision of dystopia.

What goes on in a world without redemption. It is the poet, Paul Celan's vision before his suicide, pared down to no possibility but the linguistic act itself.

These days the black widow has stopped even grinning. Her mate is merely pumped full of sugar before she proceeds to consume him.

Jack Sets Forth

After bad dreams razoring his sleep
edges of things to fall from
getting closer.

After waking to
sweat and vertigo, inoperative memories
sickness on the shifting bathroom floor.

After breakfast: cold toast
margarine and scummy coffee.

It's out on to the rain-stung
streets again.

A people to lead.

Is this then the Egypt that he has returned to? He has travelled south to a strange land and must now accept the burden of his own prophecy. There was famine in the land when Jacob headed south. And Jack was parched too. His tongue so dry it had cracked. Yet however much he drank, it made him only the thirstier for more.

He Tells His Beloved to Clear Off

Too many mornings
he has woken to crumbs on his prophecies

last night's memories of food
disintegrating wildly in the kitchen
a gin bottle dead on its side
leaking across a hand-drawn map of Zion.

Her tranquil sleep unblistered by the thousand
tiny irritations
worming underneath his skin each day.

He packed her cases for her.
Stumbled out with them into the street.
Pointed her towards the public transport
clothes-shops and supermarkets
softer fellows with less rigorous requirements.

Now back to some man's work for a change:
logic and denunciation
naming names

clearing the world of its debris.

Can an amnesiac age wake to anything but self-destruction?
The bed of Potiphar's wife is the mire of oblivion, not the true
darkness from which visions arise.

MAN OF DREAMS

I prayed that none of my sons should be burdened with
this.

But off he goes again.
Something swept down through the tides of our blood.

Throw him a wheatsheaf, he'll start telling futures.

A lean calf with its bones sticking out
stumbles on cracked Nile mud.
He's forecasting weather for the next 14 years.

Still it's a trade
in a world where specialisations are growing.

In Egypt they say a man can live handsomely
reading the dregs in the minds of the waking.
They lie on their couches
disburden themselves of their magic.

And they need a professional.
Dreams packed as tight as the tombs of their pyramids
some of those Pharaohs.

Rainer Maria Rilke, in refusing to undergo psychoanalysis, was said to remark: 'If they take away my demons, they may take away my angels too.' There is a sense in which the whole of the *Duino Elegies* can be seen as a meditation upon the meeting of angelic and human power; of how the mighty breath of the angelic would blow us away with its cyclonic force should we ever meet it face to face. In this sense Rilke's *Elegies* form a distant commentary upon Jacob's nocturnal struggle.

To have dreams is merely a form of torment. It is understanding them that brings power. So Joseph has Egyptian glory heaped upon him for being able to bring light to the Pharaoh's nocturnal foreboding. In the remarkable photographs of Berggasse 19, Freud's Viennese lair, taken by Edmund Engelmann in 1938, the ancient gods and oracles, priestesses, minotaurs and admonitory hybrids, clutter tables, shelves, bookcases, glass display boxes. Among them moves the bearded dream-teller. Outside on the streets uniformed men were already preparing to sacrifice children to the old gods. Hitler once called it the dream of a new order. It was a dream that excluded all of the descendants of Jacob, including the Doctor himself who was shortly to leave for London before the famous Viennese gemütlichkeit turned on him. The city of his practice has still to honour him with a Freudstrasse or even a Freudgasse though almost everyone else appears so honoured—for even the slightest of waltzes from that long-vanished Habsburg empire.

Homeless

Ill-shod brothers coming to the sacrifice
their clothes dispensed with,
frayed vestments gathering on icy cobbles.

Someone's nephews, someone's nieces
tiny loves, small
faces searching for the windows

in a closed compartment.
Unscheduled trains all night.
At dawn, the smoke.

PART THREE

Relatives and Singularities

Rachel's Widower

I have heard the gulls
shouting the wind down
that lifted them impeccably
over our quarrels.

And heard the wind left over from the storm
grieve on blank sands
after the gulls have gone.

I have seen the last ferryman
crossing dark water slowly at nightfall
without even that bickering net of grey feathers
trawled in the air behind him.

I have noted the shades of the months of white
the weeks of green, whole evenings of crimson
as crocus and blizzard between them
divided the time
flicked on and off like the sunlight
yet I never even blinked
at such seasonal palaver.

But now they come running from the tent:
Rachel is gone, my lord, she's gone.
Then they say darkly, Jacob
you are father to another son.

So watch me prepare
the largest piece of parchment
I ever sliced from a poor beast's back
in the middle of which I write:

Rachel, the number of her years.

Jacob's sad world is a true world now. Only the Index Boys in their mental pentagons could doubt it.

His Life in a Black Plastic Bag

7 unfinished verses
concerning chilblains and the winter cold
how resurrections interrupt
the plans of astrologers
and so many bright things passing in darkness.

3 broken toys
models of some sort.
1 book of appointments
mine it appears
discredited I might say unequivocally
by subsequent research.

5 socks
none of them matching.
1 map of the Holy Land
coloured a kind of lurid pink
with blue splotches marking
where confrontations occurred.

1 plastic memento of Penuel
an angel with wings outspread
heart glittering (a miniature battery)
through his ribcage.

2 antique postcards
one from Isaac
in a large blind scrawl:
'Why do you never write, son?

My own father damn nearly killed me
but I wrote him each week
sent snaps of the kids
holiday plans, some gossip.'

1 shawl
woven by Laban
still hugging Rachel's fragrance
that scented wind she carried with her into the grave.

1 birth certificate
signed by my brother.

1 large empty bottle.

We gather together our fragments into a heap and call it culture. And that is all right. We'll find out soon enough what we have infused with love. Sometimes when the griefs strike home we have nothing which can absorb them. Life has become flashy, metallic. It reflects everything back and we starve, trying to swallow echoes and shadows.

Jacob's life was not like that. So when his grief hit home the whole world responded to it. Everything he had ever known was significant. All the same, his own treacheries surface to assail him. How could they not?

Sic

It passes.

The white scream in the bone
scored there by the blast of man's compassion
passes.

Even the love of that
particular woman
passes
as you whisper her name it passes:

Rachel
dead love
still alive somehow.

It passes.

The elegies of the world murmur in ghostly unison: *Sic transit* . . .

How language can seem to capture the passing of what cannot be retained. And how the human psyche can still resist the blandishments of language.

Resurrection

Joseph they told me was dead is now living.

And Rachel they told me was dead is still dead.

Between His left hand
and His right hand

we fly
briefly.

Those who seek to keep their life must lose it.

But then those who do not seek to keep their life must lose it too.

Such are the symmetric options laid before us. Jacob invented asymmetry, and limped away into the dawn.

Hysteric

One who suffers reminiscences.

Dark phases of yourself, moonman, that's all
your monthly cycle.

Only the mind bleeds.

The truest speakers are the maimed ones. Those dislocated from the laughing social round speak truths and prophecies. Those visited by dark shapes and drilled by piercing voices are the chosen vessels.

Your brothers may destroy you. Esau would have done so, given his chance. Joseph's brothers had a fair try. The Bolshevik Old Guard were done to death by their erstwhile colleagues in revolution.

So what then awaits those who must tell the truth, when their lies have settled at last?

Portrait

They will arise from their entombment
in the land of crocodile and ibis
my people humble people who need little.

Always fleeing so it seems
with a stolen blessing, turning as the day turns
a struggle from nightfall to dawn.

Rainbowed in oils you will see us
at sunset, framed on your wall
a humble people often on the move.

Note that our eyes are hidden.
Hard to say whether we're laughing or crying.

They did not choose to be wanderers, however much Jack Rose might have romanticised their fate. No, the descent into Egypt, the capture in Babylon, the dispersion by elite Roman guards, the diaspora, the killings and expulsions from England, France, Spain, Germany, Italy. And then the dark crematorium at the heart of European culture. No, they did not choose to be wanderers.

They had built a most beautiful city. A city which still rests golden in everyone's mind as *the city*. Temporal and eternal. Razed to the ground it was. Abolished. But they carried their culture through the flames—a living thing like Anchises on the shoulders of Aeneas.

These were not nomads, Jack. Whatever the leanings of your waywardness might tell you. Not nomads. Citymakers turned refugees.

HIS BLESSINGS

Whatever kindnesses the blinded years to come
may offer
let them descend upon
the hands and faces of my sons
on Reuben, Simeon and Levi
on Judah, Issachar and Zebulun
on Gad on Asher and on Dan

Naphtali, Benjamin
and my beloved Joseph.

Spare a thought too
for my daughter Dinah
in the hour of her conception
and her labour.

Bless them as they go down fighting.
Small faces scattered over northern moors
the limp minutiae of life.
What should they say if they cried?
He will say
nothing.

Bless these poor men of Lancashire and Yorkshire
who heaved coal up
from the unyielding earth
who scorched without complaint
at the smelting furnace's red mouth
who shook with the cotton looms
uncherished by the mighty of this kingdom.

Who have waited for a saviour
patient in the rain.

A long time as it happens.

All who toiled and sweated and laboured for a pittance. All who shouted at the injustice meted out to their brothers and sisters and were met with imprisonment. All who are given life and then have life robbed from them by the technicians of death.

Jacob's Prophecies

Some of my children will come to no good.
Too early to tell them.
I sprinkle blessings as an old man should
behind my bearded blur of years.

Some will be king shouting their curses
as to who should be whipped
who granted a thousand rich acres
deep in the dip of majestic alluvial valleys.

God help them.

Some shall have wives they'll mistreat
others are doomed to ceaseless mistreatment by women.
Do not expect me to advise
one or the other bleak option.

And some will be hunted
through dark streets at night.
They'll get their faces rubbed in His silence.

I must forecast
dark times ahead for everyone.

Although he will glitter of course
become death gleaming
the destroyer of worlds
ready to light up the galaxy briefly
with one flash of brightness.
But then how should we say our farewells
to our increasing brood of children
fretting the night away
watering their beds with vulnerable anger?

> I prophesy
> old gaffers like me will cry out
> how they see so clearly what's coming:
> So many dark horsemen grouped on a hill.
> The darkest dream of all descending.

Once the reign of David was completed, many of the kings of Israel were corrupt. They fell from the Law. Around 600 B.C. they were captured and taken into captivity in Babylon.

And the prophets got started in earnest.

Isaiah, Jeremiah, Ezekiel and Daniel in particular told the people and the rulers what was what. For their pains they received largely persecution and disgrace. Which is the traditional way with prophets.

Jacob's seed are like those figures falling from the great flaming pod of the Hindenburg dirigible, aflame already as they fall to earth. Like lightning falling from the sky. Or sacred seed suffering bitterly in the middle region.

BACKWARDS

> Joseph has stolen your face.
> He ransacked the tomb for your features
> the least of his glances
> a blade to the heart.
>
> At noon he kisses my forehead
> and the air round his shoulders
> seems burdened with whispers.

> I'm nearly blind, love
> and I cannot tell one from another
> unless they come close where the sense of my flesh
> exonerates all my sad wits with its wisdom.
> Only Joseph's arrival I sense like
> a rising of waters or wind over corn.
>
> How they must hate him.
>
> Through the blur of my blindness I see
> a drop of water on stone
> dividing the sunlight
> and a young girl
> heaving a draught from a well.
>
> Should I approach her?
> Might she speak possibly?
> Might she droop her head once more
> in that blessèd familiar gesture?
>
> Might she know me as Jacob?

The face of a living child is a map of its ancestors. And also a possible redemption of them. Infanticide: the resolute refusal of the future.

Jacob stares at Joseph, his lost child, the child who had died, and sees his departed love, Rachel.

Even death might alter, according to the way we carry it.

Joseph leads Jacob back (blessedly) to his choices. He chose Rachel. He was given Leah but he struggled on until Rachel was given. As Joseph was given.

Jacob has lived much and seen much. More than he would care to. But this does not matter. What matters now is that, through so many lies, he has come to the truth. And this must sustain him. Even unto death.

The Interpretation of Dreams

Forget it.
Honestly.
Simply forget it.

Give it to Joseph.
Call it a gift for his Pharaoh.

Sun unseals your eyes.

For one day at least
quit jibbing and cursing.
For one day
stop ravelling back
the thread of
entanglement.

Open your creased
sewn-up face to the sun
Jack and smile.
You're half-dead already.

They mean what they mean, your dreams.
They are perfect and unapproachable
in the kingdom set aside for them.

It is Joseph's undiplomatic gift of being able to find so much valuable information in dreams which provokes his brothers' murderous ire. Bertrand Russell once claimed that it is possible that what we call waking life is merely an unusual and persistent nightmare. And Jack Rose came to sympathise strongly with this view. In Borneo if a man dreams that his wife is an adulteress, then her father is obliged to take her back. This could obviously have greatly helped Jacob the morning after his wedding to Leah.

Cicero attacked dream divination and Muhammed forbade it. There is a sense in which Freud's 'royal road to the unconscious' is inverse dream divination. The dream teller is now opening up the past instead of the future.

Those who read dreams with accuracy and grace have always been valued by the children of history.

But then it passes. The explosive destructiveness of man's compassion finally passes.

THE COUNT

> Old I am
> an old man
> plus 12 sons
> at the dry edge
> of my years
> slow to speech
> fathoming
> young schemes
> old derelictions.

We don't improve
too much
grow a little fonder
(heavy years)
of victims
brothers
crushed by land acts
chewed up by
the terrible machinery
of laughter.

Blinder I'll get
dimmer and denser
hereafter—

almost forgot
one daughter.

A diamond.

When Joseph presents Jacob to the Pharaoh, the Egyptian asks him: 'How old art thou?' And Jacob replies: 'The days of the years of my pilgrimage are an hundred and thirty years; few and evil have the days of the years of my life been, and have not attained unto the days of the years of the life of my fathers in the days of their pilgrimage.'

Our belatedness, it seems, starts right at the beginning.

Jacob has seen and done much and much of what he has seen and done has been evil. Cheated fathers, cheated brothers, murderous children, a raped daughter.

Perhaps the eyes grow dim in self-protection.

Maybe it was Jacob's good fortune to live in an age antecedent to opthalmology.

Reports

The deceased was discovered underneath the arched bridge over the canal in Wapping where he had been sleeping rough. Upon examination it was apparent that he had been dead for some time. He wore only a thin jacket and a pullover riddled with holes. He was inadequately clothed to withstand the sudden cold weather that descended on the London area during Sunday night. Cause of death: Heart failure induced by hypothermia . . .

. . . the cold spell that made life a misery for London's homeless on Sunday last also claimed an unexpected victim from the world of literature. Jack Rose, who had been living rough for some time, died under the canal bridge in Wapping which he had made his 'home'. He was the author of Nomads, a long mixed genre work on wanderers and refugees in history which had a certain cult following although it was never seen as a mainstream achievement

Its recent re-publication together with the spectacular appearance and manners of its author brought Jack Rose back into prominence in some circles. He would occasionally be seen at literary gatherings, an eccentric, growling, dishevelled figure, and not infrequently the worse for drink. At the very end of his life, though, he communed only with London's down-and-outs and himself.

He leaves a widow and two sons in Yorkshire.

Journalism seems to have replaced scripture as the obligatory daily reading for most of us, and so it is from that source that we must ask the question: What has happened to Jack? He has become a story. Well, you say, he always was. But not only for a day. For an hour. Then gone with the dead trees that provided the pulp. To be blown down the street once more.

My Son's Coat

Powders of indigo, prussian and cobalt—
winter mourning clothes
something to tide you over till
strawberry's figment of summer
will wash down the decks
its rain streaks sugared with blood.

Purple murex
pipes its grandiloquent church talk
to a shoal of shivering mirrors
a scatter of lanterns breaking up
beneath night seas.

Ultramarine's the sound of seething waters
foaming at something still parched
called burnt sienna
and over where the mountain thirsted, ochre
a hue of camel in the sun, well-brushed.

Red comes minus its words.
Vermilion's a pulse of flame
amongst carrion membranes.

Damask of course is no sooner spoken
than blown.

Salmon, the sun's glass splinter
searing your eye for a second
then an amethyst stain, half flare half shadow
reminds me of dawn.

A white as of milk
a gold as of honey
green for the fresh generations
and silver for scything.

Joseph's coat
stitched by his doting old father
another dreamer
turned rainbow-maker
in these late dark days.

The coat Jacob stitches for Joseph is like the rainbow covenant. And it is handed back stained with blood by the treacherous brothers. Jack Rose knew well enough that men die even today for lack of a coat.

OBIT.

Jack the Lad is gone
the turnip fellah
who had a candle flaring
where his eyes might be.

Down by the sad canal
amidst driftwood, cigarette ends
dead fish silvering his journey
he turned up his toes to the moon.

In search of a brother
with whom he might share a flame and a bottle.

Requiescat.

What difference does it make if this one perished in London's East End should be some quondam poet of resurrected notoriety?

It makes no difference of course. No difference and every difference.

Behind all of them lie the broken families. Families they broke or were broken by. They all seek impossible brotherhoods and warm oblivion. They are the utopians of the road, of the urinous shelter, of the defunct canal.

They plead and cajole and we largely ignore them.

In the old song 'Always lift him up' are sung the words:

> *Just remember he's some mother's precious darlin'*
> *Always lift him up and never put him down*

They lifted Jack up finally—on to a stretcher. But he was already stiff by then.

Genesis

Adam, old androgyne, inventor of genders.
His sin was the splitting.
He divorced my Shekinah and walled up the garden
(they kept it all out of the papers).

We might begin again here
naming the stones that he used.

Not on this mountain
nor in Jerusalem
but in spirit and in truth.

Epilogue

Apologia

Someone scooped me with a splash
out of an anthracite well.

Sprinkled my dark with his stars.

One of them smashed me down there
left his fist like a womb in my body.

This one betrayed me a husband
and that one a son.

Already an authorised voice at a lectern
is telling them tales
about how a well
swallowed once a nightfull of stars at a gulp
yet contrived to stay moleskinned with dark.

It is water merely, blackened silver
the poisonous mirror
a splinter of ice on your tongue before dawn.

Something to ease your distemper.

But before you mutter menaces
about this Jacob character
this sly conniving bastard and his clever myths
remember:

Like yourself I did things as I had to
getting by mostly one day to the next.

Went to the well
as you did
when too parched to stay elsewhere.

Prayed that my eyes
like your own
might grow bright at the end
with the glittering days still to come.

www.ingramcontent.com/pod-product-compliance
Lightning Source LLC
Chambersburg PA
CBHW031156160426
43193CB00008B/385